BEFORE USING...

 Before using this book, please read the guidelines inside the back cover. For a free copy of the detailed guidelines go to www.hunterhouse.com or call the ordering number below.

 To prevent bleed-through, it is recommended that water-based, rather than spirit-based, markers or pens be used in this Workbook.

I SAW IT HAPPEN

A Hunter House Growth and Recovery Workbook
by Wendy Deaton, M.A., M.F.C.C.
Series consultant: Kendall Johnson, Ph.D.
Illustrated by Cecilia Bowman

ISBN-10: 1-63026-818-6   ISBN-13: 978-1-63026-818-3

ORDERING INFORMATION

Additional copies of this and other Growth and Recovery Workbooks may be obtained from Hunter House. Bulk discounts are available for professional offices and recognized organizations.

All single workbooks: $11.95

THE GROWTH AND RECOVERY WORKBOOKS (GROW) SERIES

A creative, child-friendly program designed for use with elementary-school children, filled with original exercises to foster healing, self-understanding, and optimal growth.

Workbooks for children ages 9–12 include:

No More Hurt—provides a safe place for children who have been physically or sexually abused to explore and share their feelings

Living with My Family—helps children traumatized by domestic violence and family fights to identify and express their fears

Someone I Love Died—for children who have lost a loved one and who are dealing with grief, loss, and helplessness

A Separation in My Family—for children whose parents are separating or have already separated or divorced

Drinking and Drugs in My Family—for children who have family members who engage in regular alcohol and substance abuse

I Am a Survivor—for children who have survived an accident or fire, or a natural disaster such as a flood, hurricane, or earthquake

I Saw It Happen—for children who have witnessed a traumatic event such as a shooting at school, a frightening accident, or other violence

Workbooks for children ages 6–10 include:

**My Own Thoughts and Feelings (for Girls);
My Own Thoughts and Feelings (for Boys)**—for exploring suspected trauma and early symptoms of depression, low self-esteem, family conflict, maladjustment, and nonspecific dysfunction

My Own Thoughts on Stopping the Hurt—for exploring suspected trauma and communicating with young children who may have suffered physical or sexual abuse

We welcome suggestions for new and needed workbooks

DISCLAIMER

This book is intended as a treatment tool for use in a therapeutic setting. It is not intended to be utilized for diagnostic or investigative purposes. It is not designed for and should not be recommended or suggested for use in any unsupervised or self-help or self-therapy setting, group, or situation whatsoever. Any professionals who use this book are exercising their own professional judgment and take full responsibility for doing so.

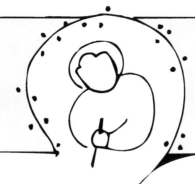

You are a special person

Write or draw your name here

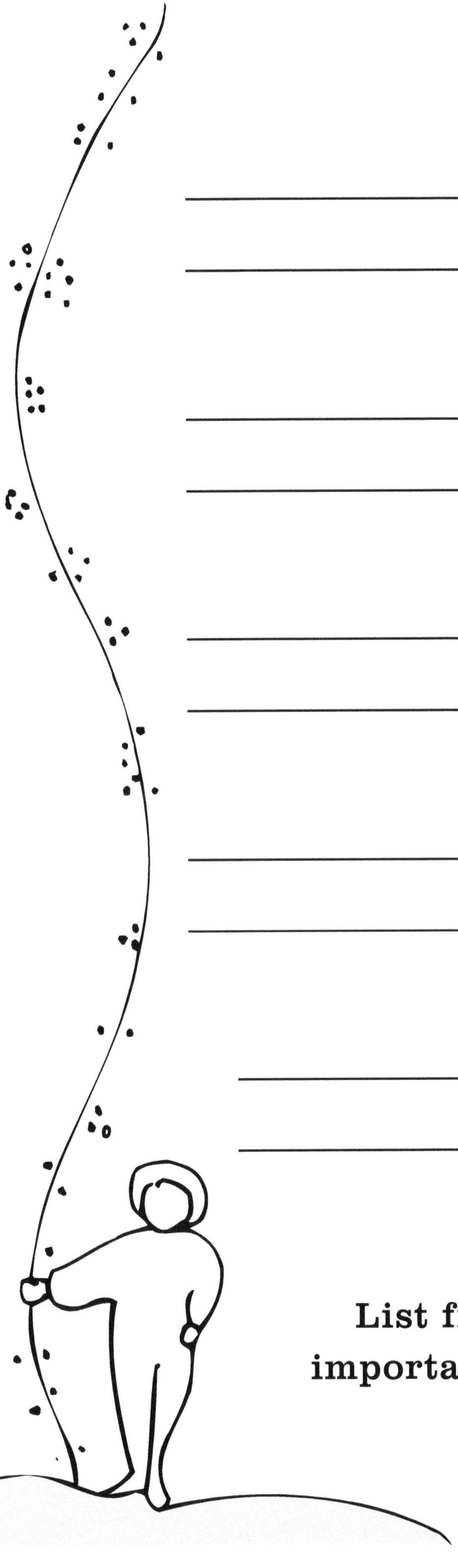

_____

_____

_____

_____

_____

_____

_____

_____

**List five things that are
important to know about you**

Draw a picture of how you feel today

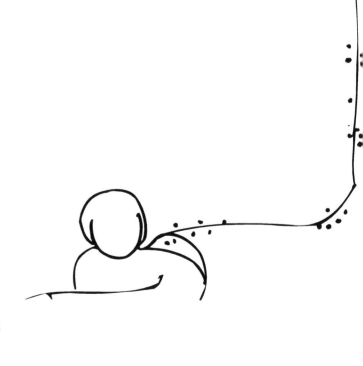

You have a special name.

Now you are called a "witness."
A witness is someone who has seen
something important, scary, or
exciting, like:

- an accident

- a shooting

- a kidnapping

- a fire

- or something else

This is your book. In it you can
tell about what happened.

4

Tell about what you saw happen here

_____

_____

_____

_____

_____

_____

_____

_____

_____

_____

_____

_____

_____

_____

Draw pictures to show
what happened

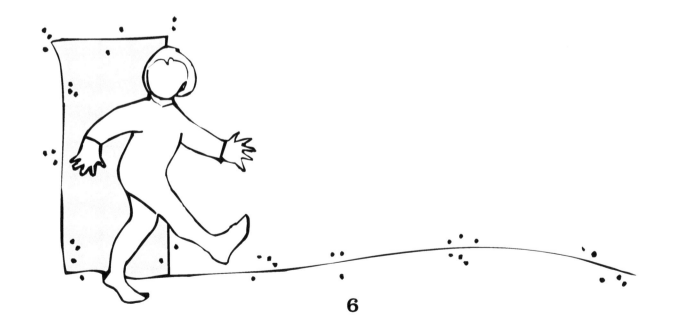

Sometimes it is hard to remember everything you saw or all the things that happened to you

This list may help you remember some of the things you saw and heard when you were a witness. Check all the words that make you think about what happened:

shooting	a big boom	a police officer
a building	broken glass	an airplane
a helicopter	a stranger	people screaming
someone hurt	the sidewalk	a person's body
a lake	a knife	the beach
a rope	a firefighter	an ambulance
windows	blood	people crying
guns	a car	

Write down any other words that remind you of what happened

_____

_____

_____

_____

_____

Draw a picture that shows what the noises sounded like

8

Draw a picture of something scary or exciting that you saw.

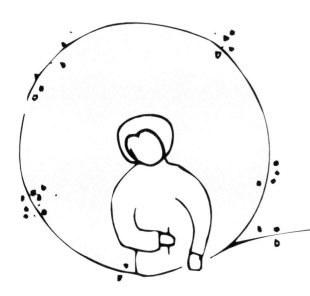

Here are some things that
witnesses say they felt
while they were watching:

"I felt like running"

"My heart pounded out of my chest"

"I wanted to scream"

"I was scared"

"I was angry"

"I was excited"

"My head hurt"

"I wanted to help"

"I wanted to hurt someone"

Write how you felt when you were a witness

_____

_____

_____

_____

_____

Draw a picture to show how you felt when you saw it happen

You saw something happen at your school, your house, the park where you play, or maybe in the street near where you live.

Write about the place where it happened

Draw or write about how you feel about that place now

Can you feel safe at this place now?

What do you need to help you feel safe?

Make a list of things you need to feel safe in the place where it happened

_____

_____

_____

_____

_____

_____

_____

_____

_____

Write about any other places where you don't feel safe

home   school   a store

a bus   the beach   a car

a lake   the park   other houses

a restaurant   indoors   outdoors

someplace else:

_____

_____

_____

Make a list of what you need to feel safe in these places

_____

_____

_____

_____

14

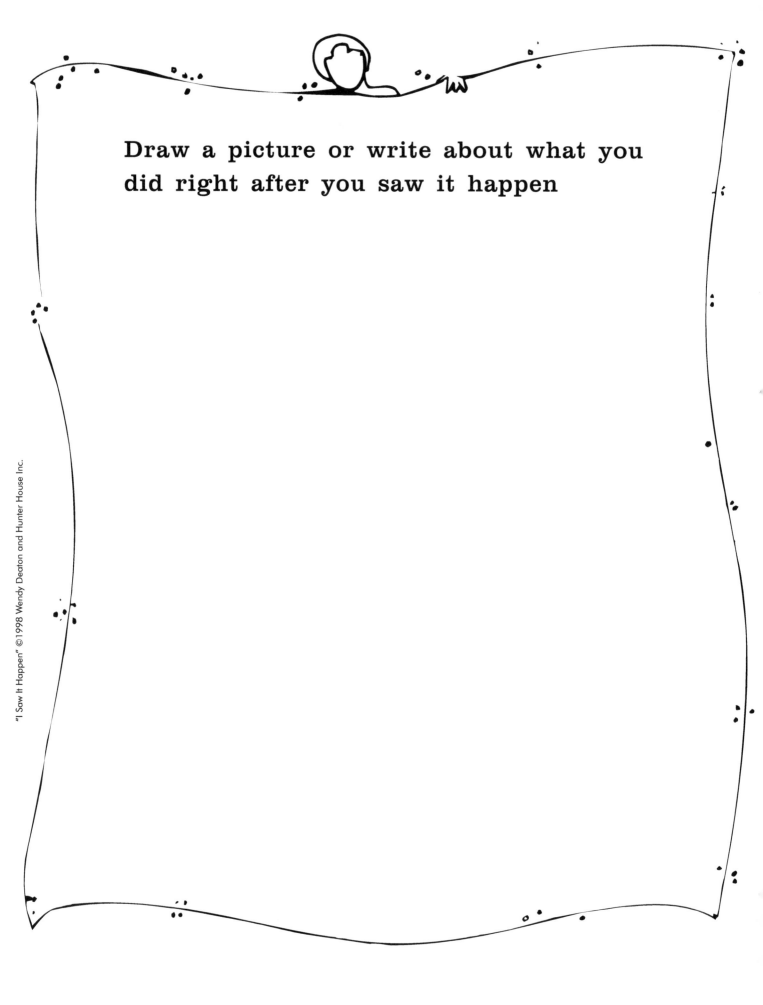

Draw a picture or write about what you did right after you saw it happen

Some witnesses feel as if what happened was their fault. Some feel they should have been able to stop what happened.

Write about any feelings you have about being responsible for causing or not stopping what happened.

_____

_____

_____

_____

_____

_____

What happened was not your fault. You would have stopped it if you could, but you were not in control. Forgive yourself for not being the person who could fix what happened.

After you are a witness, sometimes there are things that bother you. Check anything on this list that bothers you now.

sudden noises	things falling
sirens	going outside
bridges	playgrounds
cars or buses	staying in closed place
airplanes	things breaking
the dark	beaches or lakes
helicopters	people yelling
bright lights	

Write about any other things that bother you

_____

_____

_____

_____

_____

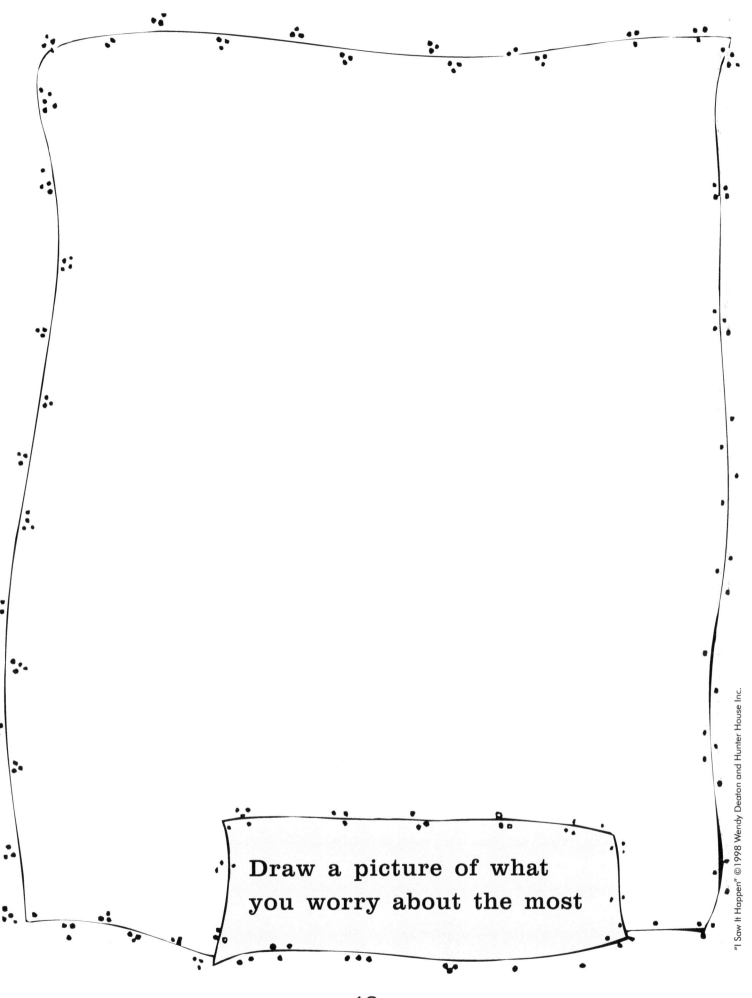

Draw a picture of what you worry about the most

If you could change anything about what happened, what would you change?

Write or draw a picture to show how you would change what happened

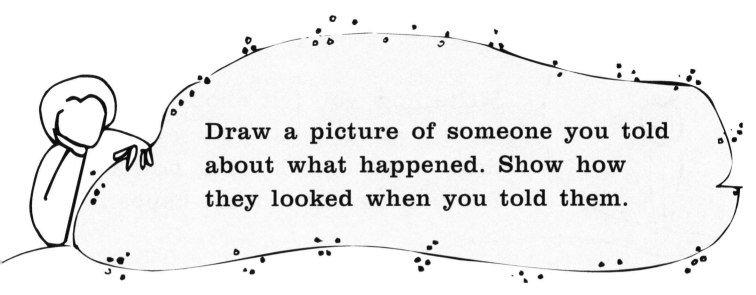

Draw a picture of someone you told about what happened. Show how they looked when you told them.

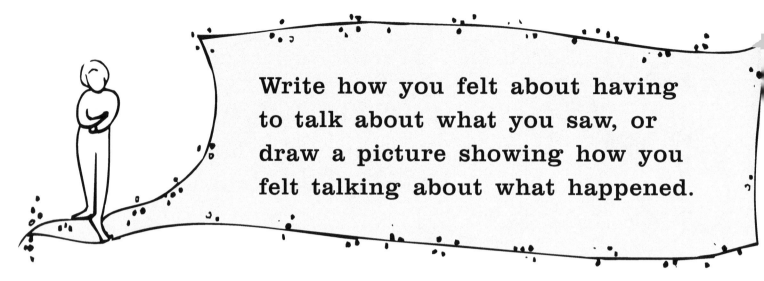

Write how you felt about having to talk about what you saw, or draw a picture showing how you felt talking about what happened.

Sometimes being a witness can change you

Write about any changes that have happened to you because you were a witness

_____

_____

_____

_____

_____

_____

_____

_____

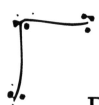

Draw a picture of you
before you were a witness

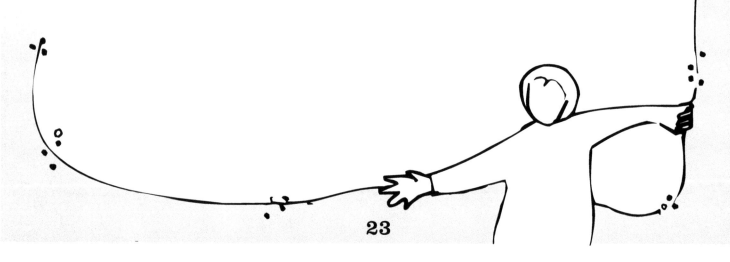

Draw a picture of you right
after you were a witness

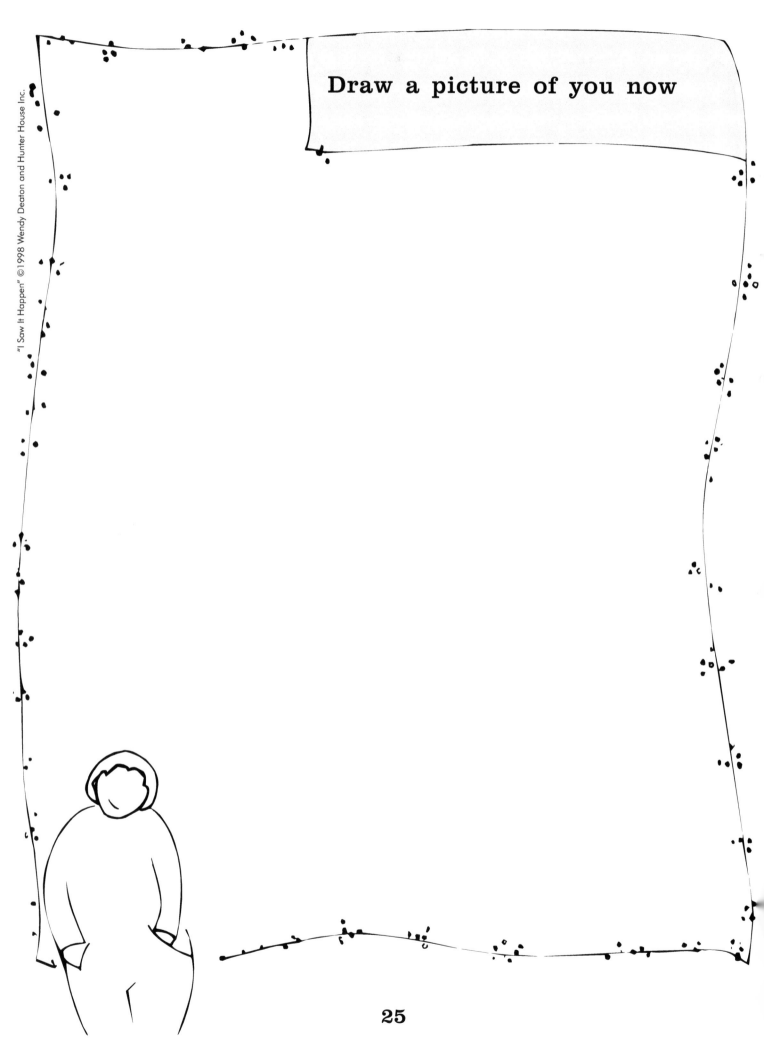

Draw a picture of you now

Being a witness may give you
bad dreams

Write or draw a picture to show
any bad dreams you have had
about what happened

Write about what you do when you have a bad dream

_____

_____

_____

_____

_____

_____

_____

_____

_____

_____

Write or draw a story about
one thing you remember most,
something that happened that was
funny or scary or exciting

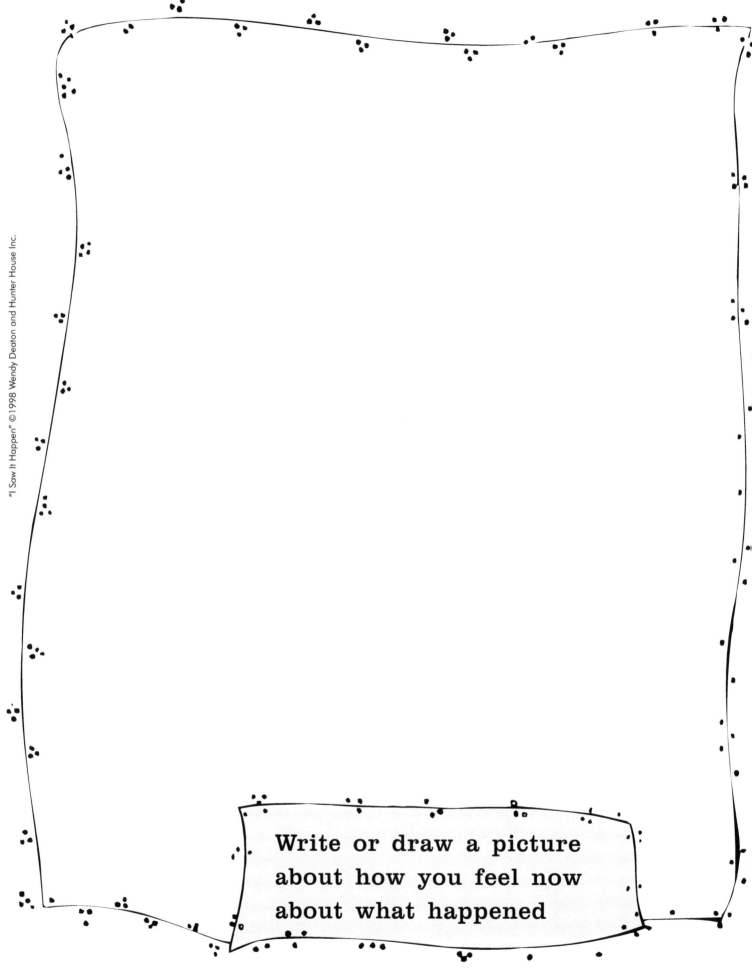

Write or draw a picture
about how you feel now
about what happened

_____

_____

_____

_____

_____

_____

_____

_____

_____

_____

Make a list of people you can talk to about what happened. Try to pick people who can help you feel better about what happened.

30

Write about something good you've learned from being a witness

_____

_____

_____

_____

_____

Make a list of things you can do to help yourself or someone else if you witness something happening in the future

_____

_____

_____

_____

_____

Make a list of five good things in your life now

_____

_____

_____

_____

_____

Write three wishes you have for the future

_____

_____

_____

PLEASE READ THIS...

This is a brief guide to the design and use of the Growth and Recovery (GROW) workbooks from Hunter House. It is excerpted from detailed guidelines that can be downloaded from www.hunterhouse.com or are available free through the mail by calling the ordering number at the bottom of the page. Please consult the detailed guidelines before using this workbook for the first time.

GROW workbooks provide a way to open up communication with children who are not able to or who are reluctant to talk about a traumatic experience. They are not self-help books and are not designed for guardians or parents to use on their own with children. They address sensitive issues, and a child's recovery and healing require the safety, structured approach, and insight provided by a trained professional.

Each therapist will bring her own originality, creativity, and experience to the interaction and may adapt the tasks and activities in the workbooks, using other materials and activities. With less verbally oriented children, the use of art therapy or music or video may be recommended, or certain exercises may be conducted in groups.

Each pair of facing pages in the workbook provides the focus for a therapeutic "movement" that may take up one session. However, more than one movement can be made in a single session or several sessions may be devoted to a single movement. Children should be allowed to move through the process at their own pace. If a child finds a task too "hot" to approach, the therapist can return to it later. When something is fruitful it can be pursued with extended tasks.

While a therapist is free to select the order of activities for each child, the exercises are laid out in a progression based on the principles of critical incident stress management:

- initial exercises focus on building the therapeutic alliance
- the child is then led to relate an overview of the experience
- this is deepened by a "sensory-unpacking" designed to access and recover traumatic memories
- family experiences and changed living conditions, if any, are explored
- emotions are encouraged, explored, and validated.
- delayed reactions are dealt with, and resources are explored.
- the experience is integrated into the child's life through a series of strength-building exercises.

Specific pages in the GROW workbooks are cross-referenced to Dr. Kendall Johnson's book *Trauma in the Lives of Children* (Hunter House, Alameda, 1998). This provides additional information on the treatment of traumatized children.

The content of the workbooks should be shared with parents or significant adults only when the child feels ready for it and if it is therapeutically wise. Workbooks should not be given to children to take home until the therapeutic process is completed according to the therapist's satisfaction.

Although this series of workbooks was written for school-age children, the tasks are adaptable for use with younger children and adolescents.

Detailed guidelines are available for each GROW workbook (see list on front inside cover).

Printed in the USA
CPSIA information can be obtained
at www.ICGtesting.com
JSHW052014140824
68134JS00006B/112